Kindness

by Clement Portlander

Original title:
Kindness

Editor: Kristo Villem
ISBN 978-9916-721-84-1

If a person seems wicked, do not cast him away. Awaken him with your words, elevate him with your deeds, repay his injury with your kindness...
Lao Tzu

No one is more cherished in this world than
someone who lightens the burden of another...
Author Unknown

Kindness, I've discovered, is everything in life...
Isaac Bashevis Singer
Voltaire

No act of kindness, no matter how small, is ever wasted...
Aesop

If you can’t feed a hundred people, then feed just one...

Mother Teresa

Whenever there is a human being, there is an opportunity for a kindness...
Seneca

The more you extend kindness to yourself, the more it will become your automatic response to others...
Wayne Dyer

Stay healthy, eat right and most importantly, be kind to all...

Tho Nguyen

Kind words are the music of the world...
F. W. Faber

Be kind whenever possible. It is always possible...
Dalai Lama

He who sows courtesy, reaps friendship; he who
plants kindness, gathers love...
Saint Basil

A little thought and a little kindness are often worth more than a great deal of money...
John Ruskin

Be kind, for everyone you meet is fighting a hard battle…
Plato

Kind words can be short and easy to speak, but
their echoes are truly endless...
Mother Teresa

The best portion of a good man's life: his little, nameless unremembered acts of kindness and love...
William Wordsworth

A warm smile is the universal language of kindness...
William Arthur Ward

Carry out a random act of kindness, with no expectation of reward, safe in the knowledge that one day someone might do the same for you...
Princess Diana

Whether one believes in a religion or not, and whether one believes in rebirth or not, there isn't anyone who doesn't appreciate kindness and compassion...

Dalai Lama

Choose to be kind over being right and you'll be right everytime...
Richard Carlson

Kindness is a language which the deaf can hear and the blind can see...

Mark Twain

You cannot do a kindness too soon, for you never know how soon it will be too late...
Ralph Waldo Emerson

CPSIA information can be obtained
at www.ICGtesting.com
Printed in the USA
LVHW070933230223
740230LV00009B/121

9 789916 721841